BASHING BOREDOM

A GUIDE TO ENGAGING STUDENTS IN THE MODERN CLASSROOM

ANDRA BOSTIC & SARAH MURPHY

Principal
PRINCIPLES
United States of America

Email: educationtailored@gmail.com
Webpage: www.educationtailored.com

Ordering Information:
Quantity sales. Special discounts are available on quantity purchases by corporations, associations, and others. For details, contact the "Special Sales Department" at the address above.

Bashing Boredom/ Bostic and Murphy. —1st ed.
ISBN 979-8-9885231-2-3

Table of Contents

DEDICATION   **5**

INTRODUCTION   **7**

WHAT IS ENGAGEMENT AND WHY SHOULD I FOCUS ON IT?   **11**

DEFINING ENGAGEMENT   13
BENEFITS   14
    Academic Benefits   *14*
    Behavioral Benefits   *16*
    Teacher Benefits   *17*
FINAL THOUGHTS   18

THE ART OF DIFFERENTIATION   **19**

ABILITY   20
LEARNING STYLES   22
    Visual   *23*
    Auditory   *23*
    Kinesthetic   *24*
LEVEL OF SUPPORT   24
    Behavior   *27*
FINAL THOUGHTS   29

WHERE DO I START, AND HOW DO I PLAN?   **31**

CLASSROOM CLIMATE AND COMMUNITY   32
    Creating a Visually Appealing Classroom   *34*
    Building Strong Relationships   *34*
    Setting and Maintaining Expectations   *36*
STUDENT INTERESTS   38
    Individual Interests   *39*
    Learning Preferences   *41*
EFFECTIVE INSTRUCTIONAL BLOCK   42
PLANNING LESSONS   43
BIG IDEAS AND REAL-WORLD CONNECTIONS   44
WORK SMARTER, NOT HARDER   46
FINAL THOUGHTS   49

WHOLE GROUP INSTRUCTION   **51**

THINGS TO REMEMBER AS YOU PLAN FOR WHOLE GROUP INSTRUCTION   53

STRATEGIES FOR WHOLE GROUP INSTRUCTION 54
Signaling 54
Think-Pair-Share 57
Random Reporter 60
Interactive Modeling 61
Gradual Release 64
Table Talk 65
Ball Toss 67
Chalkboard Splash 69
FINAL THOUGHTS 72

COOPERATIVE PRACTICE **73**

DIFFERENTIATION 75
THINGS TO REMEMBER AS YOU PLAN FOR COOPERATIVE PRACTICE 78
STRATEGIES FOR COOPERATIVE PRACTICE 79
Games 79
Task Cards 84
Jigsaw 86
Worksheets 89
Gallery Walk 93
Graffiti Walk 95
Pass the Paper 98
FINAL THOUGHTS 100

INDEPENDENT PRACTICE **103**

THINGS TO REMEMBER AS YOU PLAN FOR INDEPENDENT PRACTICE 106
STRATEGIES FOR INDEPENDENT PRACTICE 107
Entry Tasks 107
Exit Tickets 110
Choice Boards 113
Assessments 116
FINAL THOUGHTS 117

BEYOND THE BLOCK ENGAGEMENT STRATEGIES **119**

CLASSROOM TRANSFORMATIONS 120
Themed Transformations 123
Experience Transformations 124
Aligned Transformations 125
FLEXIBLE CLASSROOM ENVIRONMENT 125
Seating 126
Organization 129
Atmosphere 130

Centers and Rotations	*131*
Planning	*132*
Grouping	*133*
PHYSICAL ORGANIZATION	134
FINAL THOUGHTS	138
THE MAGIC OF ENGAGEMENT	**139**
THE MAGICAL CLASSROOM	140
Magical Tips and Misconceptions	*142*
Outside the Magic	*146*
FINAL THOUGHTS	147
ABOUT THE AUTHORS	**149**

DEDICATION

We dedicate this book to the tireless heroes who are busy shaping minds and fostering a love for learning in their students. We hope this book serves as a humble tribute to the countless hours you spend planning lessons, building relationships, and turning ordinary moments into extraordinary memories.
We also want to thank our families for supporting us and allowing us to chase our crazy dreams!

INTRODUCTION

Over the years, as we've been teaching, coaching, mentoring, and observing, we have visited many classrooms. These classrooms vary across grade levels, content areas, and even states. Throughout these visits, we began to notice consistencies: students frequently asked to leave and go to the bathroom; students were on their devices, students were having sidebar conversations, there were worksheets upon worksheets for them to complete, and there was so much teacher talk. Test scores were low, students weren't growing, teachers were exhausted, and everyone was frustrated. It became obvious that engagement was low and boredom was rampant—for everyone. This may come as no surprise to many of you, and others may disagree, but we believe that students who are bored and unengaged cannot reach their full potential in today's modern classroom.

The media has portrayed classrooms as environments where teachers lecture, and students listen. Watch any movie or show in the last twenty years, and you will see classrooms full of the "sit and get" method. This isn't a realistic depiction of school today, and that method of teaching doesn't cater to the modern student. Don't get us wrong: direct teaching is important and has a place in meaningful instruction. However, after a while, this type of instruction becomes ineffective, students become bored, and, as we previously stated, bored students aren't meeting their full potential. Modern classrooms need to change the face of education. Students learn best when they are engaged, actively participating, and interacting with their peers and the material being taught to them.

Student engagement is a vast topic, and there are many ways to achieve it. In this book, we will take you through the process of planning engaging instruction, tackle the hurdles and challenges that come with engagement, and take a deep dive into the strategies that get students engaged. Our goal is that you finish this book with the tools and strategies you need to bash boredom and improve student engagement in your own classroom. We also hope this book keeps you engaged and provides you with everything you need to be successful with your students. You will find opportunities for reflection, resources, visuals, and links to support you along the way!

WHAT IS ENGAGEMENT AND WHY SHOULD I FOCUS ON IT?

"It's better to be absolutely ridiculous than absolutely boring." -Marilyn Monroe

Student engagement should be a top priority in any classroom. Students who are engaged are going to have more ownership, success, and desire for their learning. Their level of engagement often determines their overall feelings about school. If you reflect on your own memories of school, most people tend to remember times when they were either very bored or highly engaged. Although we (the authors) never taught together, both of our classrooms were always places where students were engaged. We naturally used happy memories from our own school days to give our students the same feeling of excitement and a love of learning. We also had plenty of boring memories, and we were determined not to be remembered that way!

I vividly remember a 6th-grade social studies lesson on immigration. The students were tasked with getting from one classroom to the other to represent the way immigrants traveled from their home country to America. We had to make it through simulated travel hardships, medical testing, academic testing, and more. Teachers and paraprofessionals ran various stations that represented each of these immigration hardships. Many students never made it to the next classroom, representing the reality of immigrants.

I remember failing and not making it next door to America and being so disappointed. This lesson created an experience that accurately depicted this concept so well that I still remember it over 20 years later!

-Sarah

Before we dive into details and strategies, we want to ensure an understanding of what engagement truly is and what it looks like. We will also highlight all the benefits of student engagement that may be unknown, overlooked, or dismissed. We want to fully explore the impact of student engagement so you can begin to build a toolkit full of tips, strategies, and ideas that can be used right away. Engaging students can be one of the most powerful ways to ensure your students are successful academically while also creating positive memories that they will carry with them for years after they leave your classroom.

DEFINING ENGAGEMENT

We define student engagement as the amount of attention, interest, effort, and accountability students give to an instructional task. By engaging students, you not only increase attentiveness but also create active learners who contribute to the development of a positive classroom climate. As you look around your classroom, you can quickly gauge the level of student engagement. Are your students collaborating with each other, having meaningful discussions, and willing to complete activities? Or, are you constantly redirecting and having to pry for information and interaction while also chasing missing work? Creating a classroom centered around student engagement has benefits that can transform the learning experience for everyone in your room.

BENEFITS

What if focusing on one aspect of your instruction could not only change the academic performance of your students but also minimize undesirable behaviors, support SEL growth, and free up your time? In our experience, teachers don't truly understand the full impact that student engagement can have on their classroom, which is why many default to a simpler, less-engaging activity or lesson. Once you have a full grasp of all the benefits, it is easy to see the value of spending the time and energy it takes to ensure all students are engaged in the activities taking place in your classroom.

ACADEMIC BENEFITS

When thinking of the benefits of student engagement, student outcomes and academic growth are usually the first things that come to mind. However, these academic benefits go deeper than just a score on a test.

- **Active Learning:** Engaged students are more likely to actively participate in their learning, ask questions, collaborate with their peers, and seek a deeper understanding of the subject matter.

- **Academic Performance:** Students who are engaged are more likely to perform better academically. By participating in engaging and meaningful activities, students often have improved grades and test scores.

- **Motivation:** When students are engaged, they are more motivated to learn. They develop a sense of ownership for their learning and are able to see the connections in their personal lives.

- **Critical Thinking:** Student engagement promotes critical thinking skills. Students develop the ability to think critically, consider various perspectives, and apply their knowledge to real-world situations.

BEHAVIORAL BENEFITS

One of the most common complaints we hear from teachers is that their students "just won't behave." Our first question is usually, "Are they engaged?" Students usually act out when they are bored and not challenged or when they can't understand what is being taught because of an academic deficiency or learning gap. Engagement can help on both ends of this spectrum. When students are busy with meaningful, collaborative, and appropriate work, behaviors tend to diminish.

- **Positive Classroom Climate:** A classroom with engaged students often fosters a positive environment where students feel they are valued and belong.

- **Reduced Behavioral Issues:** When students are engaged in what they are asked to do, they are more likely to stay on task, to complete assignments, and to work with their peers in a positive, productive way.

- **Social and Emotional Development:** Engaging activities allow students to learn how to work with a team or group. These collaborative opportunities help students acquire leadership skills and strengthen their ability to participate in discussions as both the speaker and the listener. Group projects, partner work, and cooperative learning also allow students to feel a sense of belonging or purpose.

TEACHER BENEFITS

When your students are engaged in the activities you have planned, they aren't coming to you with constant questions, becoming distractions, or being off task. You have aligned with their interests, learning styles, and ability levels, and you've given them an activity that they can (and want to) complete independently, creating many benefits for you as their teacher.

- **Freedom:** When instruction is centered around student engagement, teachers have more freedom to pull small groups, conference with students, and provide extension.

- **Satisfaction:** Teachers feel more success and satisfaction when their students are engaged. They are able to give each student what they need and see growth academically, socially, and behaviorally.

- **Energy:** Instead of attempting to keep the attention of a group of 20+ students, now you get to work in smaller, controlled settings where real learning and growth can occur. You spend less of your time trying to perform, and you get to turn over the real workload to your students.

FINAL THOUGHTS

By prioritizing student engagement, teachers can create a dynamic, inclusive learning environment that promotes academic and behavioral growth, benefiting both students and teachers. Engaged students are more likely to be motivated, attentive, and invested in their education, leading to improved academic achievement, social-emotional growth, and long-term success. As we move forward in this book, we will take a deeper dive into strategies and practical approaches to cultivate student engagement, ensuring that every student has the opportunity to thrive and reach their full potential.

THE ART OF DIFFERENTIATION

"If a child can't learn the way we teach, maybe we should teach the way they learn." – *Ignacio Estrada*

In today's diverse classrooms, students come with a wide range of ability levels, learning styles, interests, and backgrounds. As teachers, it is our responsibility to ensure that all students have equitable opportunities to learn and succeed. This is where the art of differentiation comes into play.

Differentiation is an instructional strategy that recognizes and accommodates the unique needs of individual learners, enabling teachers to create inclusive and engaging learning environments.

The purpose of differentiation is to provide students with different pathways to success. These pathways ensure students are appropriately challenged, supported, and engaged. By providing students with instruction and activities that meet their needs and align with their interests, teachers can maximize student potential and growth. There are many ways you can differentiate while still keeping students engaged and excited about your instruction.

ABILITY

The first, and probably most common, approach to differentiation is to adapt based on ability levels. When students are provided with varied tasks or assignments that address the same core content but offer different levels of complexity, depth, or challenge, they are able to access the material at an appropriate level and reach their personal potential. This can be accomplished in multiple ways.

- **Small Group Instruction:** Small groups can be created based on similar ability levels. When you are running small groups and rotations, think about the order of activities for each group. For example, your higher ability groups can easily start at an independent activity, while lower groups would benefit from starting with you.

- **Tiered Activities:** Activities can be the same for students but leveled to meet their individual needs. Students shouldn't realize the differences are based on ability. For example, switch which color is assigned to groups (red isn't always low and green isn't always high) or create activities that follow

  TIERED FOOD TRUCK ACTIVITY

  the same theme (leveled books about the Titanic, leveled shopping centers students visit).

- **Tools:** There are many tools you can use to make this process easier. Sites like Newslea are great for finding leveled passages that cover the same content but are written at different reading levels. Leveled passages allow students to meet the same comprehension objective, but the readability is at individual levels.

LEARNING STYLES

As teachers, we know all students can learn, but they may not learn the same way. Catering to the various learning styles in your classroom is another great way to differentiate. As you get to know your students and their families at the beginning of the year, hone in on each student's learning style and how they are most successful. You will find that some students are kinesthetic learners, while others are more auditory or visual. During whole group instruction, you can try to vary and incorporate all these styles. For cooperative practice or small group instruction, you want to try to provide students with choice and flexibility to meet the learning style they find most comfortable and beneficial to them. There are lots of engaging activities that can fit into each style, so students are meeting the same objective but taking different paths.

VISUAL

- Use visual aids such as charts, graphs, diagrams, or images to present information.
- Incorporate videos, animations, and slides to enhance understanding.
- Encourage color coding and highlighting for visual organization.
- Provide visual cues and prompts to reinforce concepts.
- Have students create presentations or posters to visually represent what they are learning.

AUDITORY

- Use lectures, discussions, and verbal explanations to convey information.
- Leverage audio recordings or podcasts for students to review and reinforce key skills.
- Encourage and facilitate discussions, debates, and presentations to promote active engagement.
- Provide opportunities for students to explain concepts or to teach others through conversation.

KINESTHETIC

- Incorporate hands-on activities, experiments, and manipulatives to promote active learning.
- Encourage movement and physical engagement during lessons, such as role-plays or simulations.
- Use interactive technology, virtual labs, or simulations that allow students to manipulate objects or concepts.
- Provide opportunities for students to show mastery or apply skills through creation, building, or design.

LEVEL OF SUPPORT

Differentiating instruction by level of support involves tailoring teaching strategies, materials, and approaches to meet the diverse needs of your students. It also requires a deep understanding of each student's strengths, challenges, and learning preferences. By providing appropriate support, educators can create inclusive and engaging learning environments where all students can thrive and reach their full potential.

Here are some strategies for differentiating instruction by level of support:

- **Varied Learning Materials**: Provide a variety of materials, aids, and resources for students to use for support. This can be hands-on manipulatives, interactive note pages, number lines, anchor charts, or graphic organizers. The goal of these supports is to help students access the content they are applying by providing them with various supports that help them make connections independently. When done correctly, this can help students feel successful and meet the objective of your lesson.

- **Scaffolding**: This type of differentiation breaks lessons and content into manageable parts for students. The teacher frontloads instruction and then provides decreasing levels of support as students grasp new concepts and master new skills, slowly releasing control of the material to students.

- **Personalized Goals**: Set individualized goals with students based on their abilities, current performance, and interests. This helps them have a roadmap for where they are going and a visual for their progress. Setting these types of goals also helps develop intrinsic motivation for students.

- **Individualized Support:** Provide one-on-one assistance when needed; this can take place through teacher-student conferences or direct reteaching to address specific learning needs. This is the most intensive support and allows planning and time management to schedule time for individual or small groups of students. This can often be accomplished with the support of SPED teachers, specialists, or aides.

STUDENT GOAL SETTING

BEHAVIOR

Differentiation can also be focused on behavior. This type of differentiation involves tailoring teaching strategies and supports to address the unique behavioral needs of individual students. We know students exhibit a wide range of behaviors, and it can be helpful to provide

CLASSROOM MANAGEMENT

targeted interventions and supports to promote positive behavior and academic success.

- **Clear Expectations**: Establish clear and explicit behavior expectations and rules in the classroom from day one. Make sure you are consistent and provide visual reminders to reinforce them. Ensure that students understand the expectations and the consequences of both positive and negative behaviors. Include students in the process as much as possible; the more input and ownership they have, the more willing they will be to adhere to the expectations and understand why they are in place.

- **Behavior Contracts**: Develop behavior contracts or agreements with students who require additional support. These contracts outline specific behavior goals, rewards/incentives for meeting those goals, and consequences for not meeting them. Contracts provide personalized support to meet the needs of individual students.

- **Individual Behavior Plans**: Create individualized behavior plans for students who require more intensive support. These plans typically involve collaborating with the family, administration, and behavior specialists or counselors. The plans identify specific behavior goals, strategies for addressing challenging behaviors, and specific action plans or steps.

- **Social-Emotional Learning (SEL)**: Integrate and embed social-emotional learning activities into your instruction. This can help students to develop self-awareness, self-management, social skills, and responsible decision-making. By teaching strategies for emotional regulation, conflict resolution, and empathy, you promote positive behavior and can ultimately create a positive classroom climate.

SEL CHOICE BOARD

FINAL THOUGHTS

Differentiation is an art that requires a lot of work and intentionality from teachers. When it is done correctly, all students get what they need, and the classroom becomes a community of students who are able to learn, grow, and meet their full potential. When teachers create inclusive, engaging, and student-centered classrooms, every learner can thrive!

WHERE DO I START, AND HOW DO I PLAN?

"Failing to plan is planning to fail."
— Alan Lakein

Preparing for student engagement is more than just coming up with fun centers and implementing engagement strategies; it encompasses planning, knowing your students, creating a space filled with trust and encouragement, and reflecting.

Engagement requires a classroom climate and atmosphere where students feel safe, heard, and valued, and where they have a sense of belonging. Establishing the foundation for a classroom filled with student engagement takes time, effort, transparency, and intentionality. When teachers set the stage for this, engagement becomes much more effective!

CLASSROOM CLIMATE AND COMMUNITY

Classroom climate refers to the overall mood, attitude, and tone that students and teachers feel when they are in a classroom. Everyone who enters the room, including a visitor, experiences this feeling. Classroom climate and student engagement are interdependent. When students feel safe, supported, and valued, they are much more willing to participate, take risks, and fully engage in their learning.

As we all know, students and teachers spend the majority of their day at school, so ensuring you create a space where everyone can be happy and thrive for 7+ hours a day is vital. When students feel connected to their classroom, teacher, and peers, they are more engaged and invested in their learning. When a positive relationship is established between students and their teachers, students are much more likely to ask for help when they need it, comfortable sharing their struggles, and willing to take risks. A strong relationship between peers promotes collaboration, fosters teamwork, and creates a sense of trust where everyone can fail forward. Cultivating respect for the physical space is equally important, so students see the value of their classroom and work to keep it in a state that is conducive to learning. Once these relationships are established, the classroom becomes a community where everyone has a role and can reach their full potential.

We doubt there are many teachers out there who want to create a space with a negative classroom climate, but creating a positive classroom climate and community is not always easy to do. Your climate starts from day

CLIMATE SURVEY

one, and really even before. It begins as you set up your

classroom and make initial contact with your students. First impressions really are everything!

CREATING A VISUALLY APPEALING CLASSROOM

- Arrange the physical space so that students can see your instruction, access supplies and materials, collaborate with peers, and easily move around the room.
- Create a colorful, inviting space where student work, inspirational quotes, and visual aids can be displayed in order to foster a positive and stimulating environment.
- Maintain a clean, organized, and clutter-free space that promotes focus and a sense of calm. Many students come from chaotic homes and your classroom provides a space where they can truly take a deep breath and relax.

BUILDING STRONG RELATIONSHIPS

- Learn names quickly and correctly. Names are important and there is nothing worse than being called the wrong name over and over again. Students' names may have a deep connection to their family or culture.

- Share your story with students. Anytime you can make a connection or share a personal story with students, it strengthens your relationship and credibility. Also, allow time for students to share their stories and personal experiences.

- Make sure you establish a relationship with families. Try to call or send a positive note to families within the first 2 weeks of school.

- Look for ways to compliment or celebrate students. Everyone wants to feel noticed and recognized.

RELATIONSHIP STRATEGIES

SETTING AND MAINTAINING EXPECTATIONS

- Collaborate with students to develop classroom rules, norms, or expectations. Allowing students to be a part of this process gives them ownership and responsibility.

- Explicitly model expectations for students so they have a concrete understanding of what they look and sound like. Some expectations that would be beneficial to model with students are transitions (classroom and building), communication (with peers and adults), procedures (restroom, extra supplies, turning in work), clean up (end of day, center time, transitions).

- Revisit and reinforce expectations whenever necessary. If students are not following the established expectations during instruction, stop and address it on the spot. This will show them that you are committed to your structures. Losing that small amount of instructional time to be proactive will certainly pay off later.

At the beginning of my second year of teaching, my teaching partner and I decided to throw out our "Classroom Rules" and implement "Quotes to Live By." We taught 5th grade, and at that point, students were starting to resist anything labeled as a rule, and most generic rules didn't hold any real value or meaning to them anyway. We spent some time finding quotes that could help show our students how to be good people in general. Quotes like, "You are free to choose, but you are not free from the consequences of your choice," and, "Treat everyone like it's their birthday," helped students see the kind of citizens we expected our classroom to be filled with. We talked about how these weren't just things we did at school, but it was also how we treated the cashier at the grocery store or the waitress at dinner. We framed the quotes across the front of the room and frequently made them a part of our daily conversations. For example, if a student was refusing to work, I would point to the quote and tell them, "You are free to choose, but you are not free from the consequences of that choice." Another class favorite that the students liked to tell each other was, "Stop whining, start shining," to correct bad attitudes or a lack of effort. These drastically changed the way my classroom functioned, and I used them with every class and grade level I taught from that point on!

-Sarah

QUOTES TO LIVE BY

Remember, creating a positive classroom climate is an ongoing process that requires consistency, patience, and continuous effort. It sets the foundation for a supportive and engaging learning environment where students can thrive academically, socially, and emotionally.

STUDENT INTERESTS

Discovering and understanding your students' interests is an important aspect of understanding their preferences, passions, and motivations. Once you understand these things, you can use them to leverage and maximize student engagement. Student interests vary, and their impact goes much deeper than many teachers realize. When teachers take the time to learn about their students, they can personalize the learning experience, which in turn makes learning personal and engaging and shows students they are valued as individuals.

INDIVIDUAL INTERESTS

- Conducting surveys and questionnaires is a great first step in learning about your students. You can ask them about their hobbies, extracurricular activities, favorite subjects, and personal interests outside of school. Once you have an understanding of these, try to embed as many of them as you can into projects, word problems, passages, etc.

- Having one-on-one conversations with your students allows you to understand their likes, dislikes, and aspirations. Ask open-ended questions to encourage them to share their thoughts, experiences, and interests. This gives you information, while also showing your students you care about them as a person as well as a student.

- Communicate with parents or guardians to gather insights about their child's interests outside the classroom. They may provide additional information about hobbies, extracurricular activities, or previous experiences that can help you gain a deeper understanding of their child. This is also a very positive way to start the year and shows families you are invested in learning about their child and in creating a personal experience for them.

As a reading teacher, there were many times that I leveraged student interests to get them excited about reading. I had a group of sixth graders who struggled to read. This made our reading block long and often taxing. I knew many of them were interested in history, so I decided to do a novel study on *The Boy in the Striped Pajamas.* I had to read most of the novel aloud to them, but they were invested and engaged. Every day, students came in ready to begin and left begging for one more chapter. I was also able to start finding other books and passages based on the Holocaust at their level, so they could read independently and apply the comprehension skills we were learning. This changed the whole environment of our classroom; students were motivated and excited to be there. Over the years, this same strategy has worked many times. I got to know my students and what they were interested in, and knowing this information changed their whole mindset about reading and their engagement in my classroom!

-Andra

LEARNING PREFERENCES

- Understanding your student's preferred learning styles can give you clues about their interests and what engages them. Some students might be visual learners, while others may prefer an auditory or kinesthetic approach.

- As you try new activities, strategies, and approaches in your classroom, reflect on how they worked for students. Think about their academic performance, their engagement during instruction, and the overall feeling in the room. As you learn what works best for your students, you can better plan successful and effective lessons.

EFFECTIVE INSTRUCTIONAL BLOCK

As you plan meaningful and engaging lessons for your students, you have to keep in mind what an effective instructional block looks like, and then you have to consider which portion you are planning for. We believe the ideal instructional block provides students with time for whole group, cooperative, and individual practice. Typically, they are implemented in that order, but they can be arranged to meet the needs of your students, the objective, or the activity. Each piece of the instructional block serves its own purpose and lends itself to different engagement strategies. In the coming chapters, we will dive into the details of each portion of the instructional block and share some of our favorite strategies for each one.

THE EFFECTIVE INSTRUCTIONAL BLOCK

25-30%
of block time

WHOLE GROUP

This portion of the block is used to present the same information to a large group of students at one time.

50-60%
of block time

COOPERATIVE PRACTICE

This portion of the block is used to allow students to cooperatively interact, apply, and explore content.

10-25%
of block time

INDEPENDENT PRACTICE

This portion of the block is used to determine an individual understanding through intentional, independent tasks.

PLANNING LESSONS

Now that you have set the stage for student engagement and an effective instructional block, you are ready to start planning your lessons. Before you begin, we want you to remember two things: bridging the gap between your content and the real world is a very simple way to make learning engaging and relevant, and by collaborating with your team, you can lessen your workload.

BIG IDEAS AND REAL-WORLD CONNECTIONS

Each lesson or unit you plan should incorporate a real-world connection. By connecting academic concepts to real-life situations and experiences, students can better understand the relevance and applicability of what they are learning. We've all been in trainings or meetings wondering why we have to do something a certain way or how that applies to us as individuals. Students are no different, and if they can find a real-world connection or purpose, they are more likely to participate and stay engaged.

- **Lesson Hooks:** Use a real-world connection to hook your students at the beginning of a lesson or unit. Introduce the new skill or topic and help them discover all the ways it can show up in the real world. Think about ways your students may have already been exposed to or used the skill, and leverage that during your introduction.

- **Scenarios:** Use scenarios that students understand and relate to. Discuss how current skills in the classroom can be applied to solve problems or address challenges in the real world. This can be as simple as embedding these ideas into a word problem or challenging students to apply their knowledge to solve a real-world issue.

- **Guest Speakers:** Invite professionals or experts from your community to speak to your students. Guest speakers can share their experiences, offer insights, and provide real-world examples that relate to the topics being covered in class (meteorologist for weather unit, banker for money unit, newspaper editor for writing or journalism).

- **Field Trips:** Students love getting out of the classroom and connecting what they have learned at school to the real world. Field trips provide firsthand experiences and opportunities to observe real-world applications of academic concepts. There is an endless number of virtual field trips that will take your students to places they may never be able to visit.

WORK SMARTER, NOT HARDER

We know planning takes time and can sometimes feel overwhelming. You want to have the most engaging, relevant, hands-on activities you can, but you don't know where to start or how to effectively make it all happen while getting all your other work done and still having a life outside of school. This is why they call teachers superheroes. Teachers must learn how to use the resources and people around them in order to share in the workload, be creative, and use the limited time they have in the most efficient way. Below are some ways we've found to work smarter, not harder.

- **Timing:** Time is something teachers never have enough of, so you want to make sure you are making the most of every minute in your classroom. As you structure your block, think about how much time you're spending on each portion and the activities, discussions, and practice opportunities that need to fit into them. Time also needs to be considered when you are planning for rotations; if students can't complete each rotation activity in the same amount of time, you will have to consider doubling up centers, altering activities, or embedding fast finishers. It is also important that you maximize the time you're allotted in school to get as much work done as possible. Think of things students can do in order to save you time, or how to use your planning time to get more done. Students should have a part in cleaning and picking up the classroom daily and organizing materials and books. If possible, structure your planning time so that each day you have something you're responsible for getting done. For example, Thursday can be your team's designated planning day, and on Friday, you can make all your copies for the upcoming week. All these schedules and routines can help ensure your time is used effectively at school, giving you more time outside of school for yourself.

- **Collaboration:** If you plan with a team or a department, divide and conquer. Every teacher doesn't need to be making the same resources and collecting the same materials. Think about the strengths of your team and the workload each week, then delegate responsibilities to each person. This will allow everyone to have a role, and everything can get done with minimum stress and a reduced workload. Another way you can think about collaboration is using teacher assistants, paraprofessionals, volunteers, or student teachers in your classroom. Think about the most beneficial way you can collaborate and use these extra hands as resources. They can create materials, laminate, run small groups, or meet with individual students. Collaboration is the key to success.

- **Reusable Materials:** Engaging students requires more than just copying worksheets and taking notes. As you think about creating game boards, task cards, and competitive challenges for your students, keep in mind what can be created generically and reused across subjects and skills. Using card stock and laminating resources can help them last longer. You also want to think about how you will store these items, organize them, and keep them labeled. The more effort you put into them at the beginning, the less work you will have later.

- **Incorporate Technology:** In today's world, there are many resources, tools, and apps that can support you as you plan for student engagement. You have to decide where to put your energy, and leveraging today's technology to lessen your workload is a great place to start. There are many free resources on sites like *Teachers Pay Teachers* that can be used to enhance student engagement. *Canva for Educators* also gives you the ability to streamline your creative processes and make your resources and materials more engaging for free! (There are many videos outlining how to make the most of this if you need guidance.) Sites such as *Slidesmania* or *Slidesgo* have ready-made templates for slides, games, and interactive digital lessons. The themes are endless, and all you have to do is input your content!

FINAL THOUGHTS

Effectively planning for student engagement is a dynamic and intentional process that requires cultivating a positive classroom climate, knowing your students, and setting up an effective instructional block. By learning your students' interests, creating an effective instructional block, providing real-world connections, and working with your team, you can create a learning environment where students are motivated and active participants in their own learning.

While many of these things may seem overwhelming, investing time and effort into planning for student engagement is worthwhile in the long run. When your instruction is centered around engaging students, your classroom becomes a place where everyone enjoys being. You can better meet the needs of all students while helping them develop critical thinking skills, a love for learning, and the ability to apply knowledge in meaningful ways. Many of these ideas are things you already do throughout the school year. Embedding these tips and strategies involves looking at them from a different perspective. You will be surprised at how simple and impactful it really is!

WHOLE GROUP INSTRUCTION

"Tell me and I forget, teach me and I remember, involve me and I learn."

– Ben Franklin

Whole group instruction is used to deliver the same information to a large group of students at one time. It can be used to introduce new material, review concepts, or provide students with important information. This method typically encompasses lectures, discussions, presentations, demonstrations, read-alouds, and note-taking.

It is easy to fall into the habit of making whole group instruction the main teaching method in your classroom because it seems as though giving all the students the information they need at the same time is efficient. You also feel like you are maximizing your instructional time and providing students with equal access to skills and strategies. In reality, efficiency and equality often minimize effectiveness because not all students' needs are the same. In order to truly ensure you are reaching all your students, whole group instruction should only take up 25–30% of your instructional block, and the rest of the time should be used for cooperative and independent practice.

As you plan for whole group instruction, there are many strategies you can use to engage students and ensure the information being presented or reviewed is understood, applied, and retained. The ultimate goal should be that students stay engaged and interact with all the material being presented. We have all been in a sit-and-get lecture hall, and that is not only boring, but it doesn't equate to the level of learning students can achieve when they are engaged and interacting with the content being taught.

THINGS TO REMEMBER AS YOU PLAN FOR WHOLE GROUP INSTRUCTION

- **Set Expectations:** Remember that setting clear expectations and explicitly modeling each strategy is necessary before implementation.

- **Keeping a Pulse:** Remember that whole group instruction is Tier I instruction, so you may have students who need additional support at the conclusion of the lesson. Keep notes on which students seem to be struggling and will need additional support and/or leveled tasks during cooperative practice.

- **Short and Sweet:** Remember that this is not the bulk of your instructional block. This time is meant for an introduction or review of information. Use your time wisely and cover the necessary material, but make sure you leave enough time for the other portions of your block.

STRATEGIES FOR WHOLE GROUP INSTRUCTION

SIGNALING

How it works:

Signaling is a quick and easy way for teachers to gauge students' understanding and allow all students the opportunity to share their thoughts and answers. There are many different signals your students can use to interact with the lesson and to give you immediate feedback. These include:

- Thumbs Up/Thumbs Down
- Stand Up/Sit Down
- Numbered Fingers (1 finger means A, 2 fingers mean B, 3 fingers mean C, etc.)
- Sign Language
- Specific Movements
- Response Cards

Ways to implement signaling:

Signaling can be used in various ways during your instructional block to gather different types of information.

- **Preparedness:** Signaling can be used to determine if your students are prepared for the next task. Examples: Stand up if you are ready to move on. Thumbs up if you have your pencil and notebook out. Hold up 1 if you need a highlighter and 2 if you need scissors.

- **Confidence:** Signaling can be used to determine how confident your students feel about the lesson or about a strategy that has just been introduced. Examples: If you feel like you have a strategy that works for you, stand up. Thumbs up, sideways, or down: How do you feel about drawing conclusions after today's lesson? If you would like more practice with this skill before moving to independent practice, put your hands on your head.

- **Understanding:** Signaling can be used for students to share their answers and to show their level of understanding for a concept, skill, or question.

Examples: Use sign language to show me the answer you chose. Stand up if the words are synonyms, and stay seated if they are antonyms. Hold up a finger for each of the math problems you got correct on today's Kahoot.

Potential hurdles and how to prepare for them:

When you are implementing signaling, there are a few hurdles you should be prepared for. Students may be apprehensive about being completely honest with their responses in front of their peers. Therefore, you may have students who show overconfidence or a false understanding because they don't want to appear dumb in front of their peers. You may also see that students wait for their peers to answer and then copy them so they have the most popular or common answer. When you are observing and gauging your students, be on the lookout for students who may be hesitant to answer or those who are looking around for others' answers (some may blatantly copy while others are very discreet). These students may be struggling and need additional support.

The best way to address these hurdles is to ensure you have established a classroom community built on trust and support. Your students need to know that everyone in the room is going to fail at some point and that the classroom is made for learning, not perfection. Make sure you are encouraging students to take risks and to feel comfortable making mistakes. Ensure your classroom has a zero-tolerance policy for any students who laugh or joke when a peer makes a mistake or gets the wrong answer. Hold these students accountable, and take any opportunity you can to share your own mistakes and failures with them. This shows them that everyone must fail in order to grow, and no one is perfect.

THINK-PAIR-SHARE

How it works:

Think-Pair-Share is a strategy where students are posed a question or task and given time to think individually. They then discuss the answer with a partner, and finally, pairs share with the class. You can add another layer of collaboration to this process by having pairs share with another pair before the class discussion. Student partnerships can be created by simply turning to their neighbor, randomly, or by ability level.

Ways to implement Think-Pair-Share:

Think-Pair-Share can be used throughout whole group instruction for students to compare and share their thoughts and answers. The most important thing to remember as you plan for this strategy is that the question or prompt you pose needs to be accessible to all students so everyone has the opportunity to share something with their partner. Some common uses of the strategy are the following:

- **Sharing:** Students will share their answer, a strategy, or an opinion. Examples: What character changed the most throughout the story? Compare your answers and discuss what strategy you used to get there.

- **Re-Teaching:** Students restate the skill, process, or content that has just been presented. Examples: What triggered the start of the American Revolution? What are the steps to simplify a fraction?

GROUPING RESOURCE

Potential hurdles and how to prepare for them:

There are a few hurdles you may encounter as you implement Think-Pair-Share in your classroom. We often see that students don't use their individual thinking time to have an answer prepared before they talk to their partner, or that one student is more vocal and dominates the conversation. Students may also get off task and start having sidebar conversations.

These hurdles can be avoided if you model and scaffold the process at the beginning of the year or prior to students using it independently. This should include you thinking aloud and showing students how to respectfully share answers, actively listen, and stay on task. You might even want to set timers the first few times they use this strategy so students can make sure each partner has a chance to share before they discuss and compare their responses. If you find some of your students dominate the conversations or argue about who goes first, you can assign roles. Roles can be assigned by numbering partners, flipping a coin, or based on their age (older or younger). If sidebar conversations become a common issue, revisit expectations, analyze the amount of time you are allowing, or provide a mini-fast-finisher question to extend the conversation. One additional thing to consider is that if you have a diverse group of students (academically or behaviorally), you may want to think about how you will assign partnerships in order to ensure quality conversations take place.

RANDOM REPORTER

Random Reporter is a strategy used to call on students to share answers or information. Rather than calling on the same students who always raise their hands, this method gives every student a chance to answer and an opportunity to participate. It also holds students accountable and ensures all students are actively listening and involved in the lesson.

You can accomplish this with the following:

- An online spinner/wheel
- Popsicle sticks in a cup
- Apps (many like ClassDojo have this feature)

Potential hurdles and how to prepare for them:

When you are using Random Reporter in your classroom, the most common challenge is supporting students who may feel anxious or nervous about being called on if they don't know the answer. Make sure you have procedures in place for students who might require additional support to prevent potential embarrassment. This might mean having the option to "phone a friend," choosing an answer buddy, or allowing students to talk to a partner or their table group before you select a student to share. Having these supports in place will provide an even playing field for random reporting.

INTERACTIVE MODELING

How it works:

Interactive modeling is a strategy for teachers to use as they work through problems, strategies, notes, or steps. As you are modeling, use think-alouds and have students give input, identify mistakes, direct you to the next step, or explain a process. This strategy can be very beneficial to students as it keeps them engaged and allows them to truly process what the teacher is showing them because they are actively involved and interacting with the content, not just watching the teacher work or mindlessly copying notes.

Ways to implement interactive modeling:

Interactive modeling can be implemented across subject areas and is most often used during the introduction of a new skill or concept. We have also seen it used as a beneficial strategy during remediation.   Some common ways to implement interactive modeling are the following:

- **Note Taking:** Create fill-in-the-blank notes that students can work through while you introduce a skill or concept. You can also leave blank spaces for students to draw pictures that represent an idea or to work through an example problem.

- **Math Problems:** As you're working through a problem, ask students, *What should I do next? Did I do that* *correctly? What mistake did I make? You can also ask students, What strategy should we use to solve this problem?* or show them a completed problem and have them determine if it was done correctly.

- **Reading Comprehension:** As you are working through comprehension questions or skills, model how you use text evidence, reread, or summarize to determine your answer. Ask students, *What text evidence can you find to support this answer? What connection can you make with the character after reading that excerpt? What do I need to make an inference?*

- **Writing Process**: Have students edit your writing. Ask them questions like, *"What punctuation should I use here? How can I rewrite this sentence to make it sound better? I want to add this idea to my paper; which paragraph should I add it to?*

Potential hurdles and how to prepare for them:

As you implement interactive modeling into your instruction, be prepared for hurdles that you might encounter.

You may find that students don't yet have a strong enough grasp of the skill to answer your questions. To prepare for this, make sure the questions you are asking are aligned with what you have just instructed, and if students can't answer them, that means you need to reteach, so you will need to have extra examples prepared.

When students are filling in their notes, you may find that they take too much time. To avoid this, make sure that the blanks they have to fill in are straightforward and that the activities accompanying their notes can be completed quickly. This is not meant to be a lengthy process.

GRADUAL RELEASE

How it works:

The gradual release strategy is a model where teachers intentionally transfer and release information and responsibility to students. This allows you to provide intentional instruction and guide students to independence. The first step in the gradual release process is to fully model a skill or concept. It is important that you model your thinking as well as your work. Then, you ask students to give input on what you should do next while you are modeling the work. Once they have seen a few examples, you can release responsibility to the students and allow them to attempt an example with a partner or table group for support. Finally, you release full responsibility and see which students have grasped the skill and which still need additional support.

Potential hurdles and how to prepare for them:

As you use the gradual release model in your classroom, keep in mind that students may work and finish at different paces. Plan with this in mind and only give them enough time to complete the example, knowing that if students are struggling, you will need to step back in the process with the whole group or plan to pull specific students as you transition to cooperative practice.

TABLE TALK

How it works:

Table Talk is a strategy that allows students to collaboratively process information, discuss a topic, or complete a task. Students are seated in groups, and when posed with a question or topic, they discuss it with their table. This format allows all students to take an active role while also learning from their peers.

Ways to implement Table Talk:

Table Talk can be used during whole group instruction as a way for students to have quick discussions and collaborate about instructional topics. Some common uses are the following:

- **Creating a KWL or Anchor Chart:** Students will discuss what they know and want to know about a topic as a table. Then, as groups share ideas with the class, the teacher fills in a class chart.

- **Addressing a Common Mistake:** The teacher will show an example of a common mistake students made on a previous assignment. Then, at their tables, students will analyze and discuss what they believe the mistake was and how to correct it.

- **Summarizing or Recapping:** Table groups will discuss key points from instruction to summarize or recap what was presented and ensure understanding before moving to cooperative practice.

<u>Potential hurdles and how to prepare for them:</u>

When you implement Table Talk in your classroom, the most common hurdle tends to be ensuring that all students have the opportunity to share and that conversations stay on topic. Make sure the expectations set for this strategy allow everyone at the table to share if they have a response. You should also be aware of how much time you are allowing groups to talk so sidebar conversations don't occur.

BALL TOSS

<u>How it works:</u>

Students create a circle in the classroom. Then the teacher poses a question or topic and chooses a student to start. That student shares their answer and then throws a ball to a classmate. Whoever catches the ball shares their answer, and the cycle continues. The process ends when there are no more answers, repeated answers, or time is up.

Ways to implement Ball Toss:

Ball Toss is a fun, fast-paced strategy to get students thinking about a topic or listing examples for any subject area. The trick is to pose a question or topic on which students can generate multiple answers, so the process can continue long enough for all (or most) students to have a turn.

- **ELA:** This strategy can be used to have students generate antonyms, synonyms, rhyming words or word study patterns. It would also be a great way for students to list story elements, text features, or genres.

- **Math:** Ball Toss is a great way for students to apply skills like even/odd, prime/composite, or skip counting. They can continue naming examples until there is a mistake, a repeat answer, or the timer goes off.

- **Science/Social Studies:** This would be a fun way to reinforce or review any concepts that have multiple examples or parts. Students can name states, countries, continents, or capitals. It would also work well for generating examples of things like solids, liquids, or gases.

Potential hurdles and how to prepare for them:

The main challenges we see with Ball Toss are students who don't have something to share when the ball is thrown to them or students who get distracted with throwing the ball, which takes away from the objective of the activity. You can put supports in place to help students who may not have an answer, like Phone a Friend or Buddy Buzz. You will also want to set expectations for throwing the ball and remind students that intentional misuse of the ball can mean that they have to sit out and list their answers on paper while the class continues.

CHALKBOARD SPLASH

How it works:

The teacher poses a question, statement, or prompt on the board. Students quickly respond by writing a response in 15 words or less at their desk. As soon as students are ready, they come to a designated space on the board or a chart paper to write their response. This creates a collective visual of their thinking, ideas, and understanding.

Ways to implement Chalkboard Splash:

There are many ways that you can use this strategy to enhance collaboration and discussion in your classroom while also ensuring everyone participates.

- **Favorite Part or Takeaway:** This can be used for students to share their favorite part of a story or text, their favorite person from a time period or event you have been studying, or a key takeaway from the lesson.

- **Summarizing:** Chalkboard Splash can be used for students to write a summary of what they read or learned during the block.

- **Strategy:** This is a great way for students to share a strategy they used to solve a problem or come to a conclusion or answer. Then the teacher can lead a discussion based on the different strategies that were used.

- **Questions or Goals:** Students can put a question they have about a topic on the board or their goal for a unit.

- **Interactive Response:** After students share a response to the original posed question, they can respond to classmates on the board or through discussion.

Potential hurdles and how to plan for them:

As you are planning to use Chalkboard Splash in your classroom, there are a few common hurdles to be prepared for. The first hurdle many teachers face is not having a board with enough space for all students to share. This can be easily remedied by using chart paper or letting students write on a sticky note and then placing it in a designated area. The goal is for students to share; it doesn't matter if it is actually on a chalkboard or not! The other issue that often arises when implementing this strategy is the amount of time students take to develop a response. It is good practice to set a timer, and all responses stop when the timer goes off. You can even have a class goal of beating your previous time each time you do this.

FINAL THOUGHTS

We know embedding these strategies and ideas will have a large impact on your whole group instruction. We also know the nature of whole group instruction requires more teacher talk than other areas, but keeping students actively involved will strengthen your Tier I instruction, leading to higher student gains, reducing the size of your lowest group of students, and minimizing the work you and your students have to put in later.

COOPERATIVE PRACTICE

"The true strength in our classroom lies in the collaboration of learners, not the knowledge of one expert." – Unknown

Cooperative practice is the portion of your instruction when students are applying and exploring the concepts, strategies, and skills that have just been presented. During cooperative practice, students truly get what they need to be successful. Teachers should structure this time to include centers, rotations, partner work, or small group instruction. This portion of the instructional block should be hands-on and allow students to cooperatively process and apply the information that they were just given. Many teachers avoid this area of instruction because it can seem overwhelming to plan and chaotic to manage. However, if you begin the year setting expectations for cooperative practice, effectively model and allow students to practice these expectations, and then maintain and revisit them as needed, this will probably end up being everyone's favorite part of the block.

Cooperative practice should be the meat of your lesson and where you spend the most time. It allows students to maximize their time manipulating, applying, and practicing skills while you work with students who aren't quite ready for that and still need your guidance. Oftentimes, struggling students do not get what they need during whole group time because it can be difficult to stay focused and doesn't allow them enough time to process or truly understand the information being taught. This is why it is vital that you devote 50–60% of your instructional block to cooperative practice. It is the only time every student gets exactly what they need.

The ultimate goal of cooperative practice is to give students time to effectively and cooperatively practice skills with the support they need to reach their full potential. When students are given assignments they are interested in at the appropriate ability level, they will not only complete their work, but they will also be actively engaged in it. Instead of seeing bored, frustrated students, you will see students who are interacting and learning without needing constant reminders and redirections from you.

DIFFERENTIATION

As we mentioned above, cooperative practice is meant to give each student exactly what they need to grow, learn, and ultimately thrive. In order to do this, you will have to differentiate during this portion of the instructional block by focusing on groupings and leveled assignments.

Students can be grouped according to similar or mixed ability levels. Mixed-ability groups take intentionality, clearly identified roles, and assigned responsibilities. Research shows that students learn well from their peers and that reciprocal teaching is a strong instructional strategy. So, pairing lower-achieving students with higher-achieving students can be powerful when used appropriately. When doing this, make sure that the higher-achieving students don't just take over and do all the work independently. Setting expectations for each student's roles and responsibilities can help with this. Ask that each student turn in a physical copy of their own work, and assign specific students to be the explainer or dictator and another student to be the scribe. Let them know they are working together, and you expect to see and hear evidence of that taking place. On the other hand, putting students in similar ability groups can also be very effective. This allows you to change assignments, level work, pull small groups to support students' specific needs, and address learning gaps.

Leveling assignments is another great way to differentiate. Doing this allows lower-achieving students to work independently of the teacher and access the current skill with the support of their peers, which helps them gain confidence and independence while giving higher-achieving students the opportunity to extend. While this may sound daunting, there are a couple of ways you can make this process manageable.

In math, making problems simpler doesn't always mean a completely new assignment. For example, if you are teaching students to add unlike fractions, have the lower group only add fractions that can be easily changed, like thirds and sixths or fourths and eighths. The same questions can be used, but sub out the fractions. In reading, there are resources like Newsela that allow you to print off the same article at various reading levels while still using the same comprehension questions for all students.

We know this is a lot of information to take in, but differentiation is key to student engagement and success. Make sure you read the chapter we devoted to differentiation; it takes a deeper dive into this aspect of instruction so you can ensure each of your students is getting exactly what they need. When this happens, you can become a learning facilitator instead of a lecturer.

THINGS TO REMEMBER AS YOU PLAN FOR COOPERATIVE PRACTICE

- **Differentiation:** This is the point in your instructional block where you can meet each student where they are and provide them with what they need to be successful.

- **Invest in Expectations:** Cooperative practice involves a lot of moving parts. Set, practice, and maintain strong expectations to ensure you maximize this time. It is a good practice to introduce games, rotations, and centers with non-academic examples first.

- **Time Management:** In order to get through everything you have planned for this portion of the block, you will have to be focused on time. It is easy to get engaged in a game or small group activity and want just 5 more minutes, but that can throw off the whole schedule. Set timers and stick to them, especially in the beginning.

STRATEGIES FOR COOPERATIVE PRACTICE

GAMES

Ways to implement games:

Games are a great way to leverage competition in the classroom, and there are very few things you can't gamify. Depending on your goal, games can be used for review, practice, small group work, or extensions.

- **Jeopardy:** This is best used as a review game. There are many templates and premade games online that can be used right away or edited to fit your specific needs. A good practice when playing Jeopardy is to require every student, or at a minimum, every group, to answer each question. Set a timer that allows quiet group work time to determine their answer, and if the group answering gets the question wrong, allow the other groups a chance to answer and steal the points.

- **Board Games:** You can use real board games and substitute the playing cards for task cards or question cards you've created. There are also many free blank game boards available online. You can use items you have around the classroom (math connecting cubes, mini erasers, etc.) for game pieces.

- **EdTech Games:** Interactive games like Kahoot, Blooket, or Plickers allow you to make review and reinforcement of a skill fun and competitive. Each game allows you to use ready-made question sets or to upload your own. Students can complete this in teams, in partnerships, or independently against peers.

- **Trashketball:** This game is so simple yet so effective! You can use your classroom trash can or buy a couple of cheap mesh trash cans from a local store that are designated Trashketball cans (this is what I did - much cleaner). As students answer questions posed by you (on worksheets, task cards, etc.), allow them to shoot a paper ball into the trash can for points. The team with the most points wins. I always like to add an extra shot option in math class for students who get the answer and show their work!

- **Tic-Tac-Toe/Connect Four:** These games can be printed out on paper, or the real physical games can be used. Students can play these games while they are completing a worksheet or answering task cards. Once they answer the question correctly, they may make their move or take their turn.

- **BINGO:** You can make any skill or question set into an opportunity for Bingo! Anything with concrete answers can be put on a Bingo board (math problems, vocabulary, sight words, antonyms/synonyms, state capitals, etc.). Each student or team gets a board (you can find lots of ready-made sets online), and they need something to cover their spaces. Bingo can be played in pairs or individually. If typical bingo gets boring, encourage students to cover four corners, make an X, or cover the board.

- **Buzzers:** Buzzers are a fun and easy way for students to answer and share. They can make small group time much more engaging or get students excited to attend a remediation session. You can buy electronic buzzers online that light up and make sounds, or you can take a more affordable approach and let students slap the table or hold up a sign to buzz in. Regardless of the buzzer you use, students love when you turn practice time into this fast-paced response game!

- **Zip, Zop, Zap:** This is a great way to play a review game. Create a game board electronically or on poster board. The board should have 15-20 numbered spots on it. Students work in 2 teams, and as they correctly answer a question, they choose a numbered spot. Each spot has a card associated with it (behind the numbered card): Zip (+10 points), Zop (+15 points), or Zap (-10 points). You will want to change up your cards each round so students don't memorize their placement!

- **SWAT:** This game can be played in a small or large group. Start by spreading out flash cards, sight words, letters, or the answers to a series of questions on your table or board. Divide students into teams and give each team a fly swatter. Ask a question and have students take turns "swatting" the answer. Whichever team/individual has the most points after all answers have been swatted, wins.

Potential hurdles and how to prepare for them:

As you gamify your instruction, be prepared for the hurdles that may arise. Although competition is healthy and fun, it can also quickly become heated. Students need to be reminded that there is an appropriate way to handle both winning and losing, and if your classroom uses games a lot, it typically becomes routine. You may also find that the process of games can get lengthy; have procedures in place for how long a team has to answer or a timer for teams to come up with their team name (and if they don't have one, you will choose it for them). Little things like this can save a lot of wasted time.

One year, I had a group of 4th graders who were not great at sharing or losing. It caused meltdowns, arguments, and occasionally someone storming out of the door. I decided I would attempt to help the next set of teachers, and we spent our last week of school rotating through board games and other activities students brought in. We had class conversations about how to lose, how to share, and how to respect time limits. This group absolutely loved games; we just had to learn how to handle ourselves when we weren't the winners. I can't say we ended the year perfectly, but hopefully it helped those 5th grade teachers some!

-Sarah

TASK CARDS

Ways to implement task cards:

Task cards are a great way for students to practice or review a skill. You can use task cards in any subject area, and they can easily be leveled and tiered to reach all learners. The possibilities for making them engaging are almost endless!

- **Scoot:** Number each task card and place them around the room. Students each have an answer sheet and scoot around for a specific amount of time or a number of cards to complete them. They can do this independently or with a partner. Different colors can correspond to different levels or groups.

- **Board Games:** Task cards can be swapped with game cards and students can play a game as they correctly answer their cards.

- **4 Corners:** Read a task card and students go to the corner of the room that correlates with their answer (A, B, C, D). You will need to establish the corners before starting.

- **Speed Dating:** Each student is assigned a card that they know the answer to. (Make sure they are all prepared before starting.) Then, students partner up and ask each other their questions. When the timer goes off, they find a new partner and repeat the process. They can do this as many times as you want or have time for.

- **Station Work:** Incorporate task cards into your stations or rotations. Cards can be spiral reviews or based on the current skill. If students are working independently, have an answer sheet or buddy system in place in case anyone gets stuck.

Potential hurdles and how to prepare for them:

Students may complete cards at different paces, so have more cards than students, regardless of how you use them. They can also be easily lost or mixed up. If you are using multiple sets during a lesson, color code them based on skill or level. Simple organization tricks will help you manage their use and clean up much faster!

JIGSAW

How it works:

The Jigsaw strategy requires that students be a part of two teams: a "home" team and an "expert" team. Students are each assigned to a home group, and then each member is assigned to a different expert group. First, they meet with their expert group to learn about a specific topic, area, or skill. Then, they go back to their home group and explain and discuss what they learned. This method encourages responsibility and cooperation among students.

JIGSAW VISUAL

Ways to implement Jigsaw:

Jigsaw works best for subjects and ideas that students can easily self-teach using materials that the teacher provides. This can be in the form of slides, notes, books, or links. The number of students assigned to each home group needs to match the number of topics and concepts being covered.

- **Parts of a Whole**: This type of Jigsaw focuses on all the individual parts that make up a whole topic or concept. For example, the geographical regions of the USA, parts of a flower, or the steps of the Scientific Method.

- **Topic-Based Examples:** This type of Jigsaw allows students to explore a variety of people, ideas, or characteristics all centered around the same topic. For example, presidents, animal classes, or oceans.

- **Vocabulary:** This type of Jigsaw can be used to introduce or reinforce vocabulary for students. Teachers often find this helpful at the beginning of a unit or before a test.

<u>Potential hurdles and how to prepare for them:</u>

The first hurdle you should be aware of is creating equal groups that have the ability to cover everything you plan for. For example, if you were covering the planets, the ideal Jigsaw setup would require 64 students (8 students per planet). To make this more realistic, you will need to think about how you can group your students based on the numbers in your classroom. This may mean student groups are assigned to more than one topic or idea. For example, if you have 16 students, you can have 4 groups of 4, and each group would become an expert on 2 planets.

The other major hurdle you will need to be prepared for is student clarity and reliability. Students need to be able to clearly share the information they are "experts" in with the other group members and be reliable enough to bring all the new information they learn back to their home group. Consider having a note sheet or organizer that all students fill out. This helps the students organize the information they are learning so they can take it back to their group. Once back with their "home group," students continue to fill out the organizer as each member shares their expertise. At that point, the teacher can go over the key ideas students need to know. If this is already on their organizer, they should highlight it; if not, they should add it. This aligns the activity with what students may see on the test and becomes a note sheet that they can keep and refer back to.

WORKSHEETS

Ways to Implement worksheets:

We know that worksheets are the most accessible and commonly used instructional tool. They are easy to find, simple to create, and cheap to buy. We typically see worksheets used as independent work, and while we know students need rote practice and a chance to apply skills and strategies, there are ways to make worksheets engaging and intentional.

- **Competition:** There are several ways you can turn worksheets into competitions in order to give students more motivation to complete them with maximum effort and accuracy. When implementing the examples below, it is important that you, as the teacher, are available to check work, problem-solve, and keep students on task. Consider having the assignments leveled and students grouped by ability to ensure all students are able to participate.

- **Cup Stacking:** Give students a worksheet and assign questions a cup value. This can be assigned based on level of difficulty (a three-step math problem is worth three cups) or work (if you show your work or find ample text evidence, you get an extra cup). If students complete the problem correctly or show their work, they can earn cup(s). Students work with partners to complete problems/questions accurately and earn cups for their team. Once all the questions have been answered or problems have been solved, students will work with their team on a cup stacking competition. For example, the team may need to build the tallest tower or create the most unique design. Tell students about the competition, then set a timer for two minutes and allow students to build. Once time is up, creations will be judged for a "winner."

- **Tip:** Set the standard from the beginning that once the timer goes off, the cup creation your team has is the one that's getting judged, with no extra time and no redos. If you had the tallest tower and it fell to the floor with 2 seconds left, you understand that is disappointing, but time is up. This ensures no instructional time is lost, and they learn real-life lessons. They may be mad at first, but eventually, they learn that sometimes things just happen and it's okay.

- **Trashketball:** Students shoot shots of trashketball and rack up points as they correctly answer questions or accurately solve problems.

- **Chop Chop:** There are many ways that you can cut up a worksheet and use the questions to create engaging activities for your students.

- **Scoot:** Cut up the questions and place them around the room (number them for organization). Students will scoot to the different questions for an allotted amount of time.

- **Open and Solve:** Cut up the questions on a worksheet and place them into themed containers (Easter eggs, pumpkins, Christmas boxes, etc.). Students will each get a set of these to open and solve or find them around the room and answer them.

- **Task Cards:** Cut up the questions and glue them to index cards to create a set of task cards or flashcards. Students can complete these in rotations, small groups, or with a partner.

- **Scavenger Hunt:** Cut up the questions and post them around the room. For this activity, you will give students the answers to the worksheet, and they are hunting around the room to find the question that matches their answer.

Potential hurdles and how to prepare for them:

As you plan to make worksheets more engaging, you need to make sure you are still meeting the needs of all learners. You may need to have tiered worksheets or questions based on the ability level of your students. As you pair and group students for these activities, think about what procedures are in place to hold each student accountable.

GALLERY WALK

How it works:

A Gallery Walk is a way for students to get up and move while learning new material or practicing a skill. Groups of students move around the room and visit different stations. Stations are used to present new material or reinforce a skill by providing students with activities to complete or discuss (books, slides, informational packets, QR codes, videos, etc.). As students visit each station, they can fill out a guided note page or graphic organizer that you have created. This ensures alignment with your lesson objective while also holding students accountable.

Ways to Implement Gallery Walks:

Gallery Walks can be used across subjects and grade levels, accommodating different learning styles while promoting student engagement. This strategy encourages active participation, collaboration, and the exploration of multiple perspectives.

- **New Material:** Gallery Walks are a great way to introduce students to new material. You can create quick stations that introduce concepts and vocabulary, or activate background knowledge. After students have completed the walk, they will be familiar with and ready for your direct introduction of the material. This works great with topics like parts of a flower, book genres, classifying shapes, or Native American tribes.

- **Current Skills:** Students can practice the current skill in a way that gets them up and moving and collaborating with a small group. For example, if you just introduced graphing in math, each station can have a different graph or data set that students interpret and answer questions about.

- **Review:** A Gallery Walk is a great way to provide students with a review for a unit test or spiral back to previously taught skills. The stations for this format do not have to be based on the same topic but can cover multiple skills based on what you know your students need practice with.

- **Student Showcase:** This format is an alternate way to use a Gallery Walk where student work is displayed at each station for peers to visit. This can be a great way for students to show off research, projects, or presentations to their classmates!

Potential hurdles and how to prepare for them:

As you plan for Gallery Walks keep the amount of time you are planning for in mind. It is easy to create too many stations or more work than students have time for at each station. Think about the objective and align your stations with that goal. It may be helpful to set a timer for each station and to group students in a way that accommodates and meets the different ability levels in your classroom.

GRAFFITI WALK

How it works:

A Graffiti Walk is a great way for students to use their creativity and artistic abilities. Students or teams brainstorm and reflect on a topic, question, or idea individually. Then, they take their ideas and "graffiti" them on chart paper or posters around the room. Each poster corresponds to the topics or questions being posed. The first time you try this activity, students may need some visuals of what graffiti looks like. As they complete the walk, they will need to be provided with different colors to create the true effect. After students finish, you can debrief by quickly going over each poster, having students present the poster they ended on, or having students revisit each poster with their group for discussion.

Ways to implement Graffiti Walks:

Graffiti Walks can engage students in all areas of your day. This is a strategy that can easily be adapted to the needs of your classroom.

- **Academic:** Graffiti Walks can support academic instruction in your classroom by asking students to apply or give information about a specific skill or topic. For example, each poster can have a word ending or pattern, and groups would graffiti examples of each. In math, you can provide an answer to a problem, and groups would be tasked with coming up with a word problem that would have that answer.

- **Social Emotional:** Graffiti Walks can also be used to embed social-emotional checks into your instruction. You can ask how students are feeling about a particular skill or what they need to feel successful. You can also use the posters to gain an understanding of their interests, so you can use them as a reference to plan and engage students throughout the year.

- **Expectations/Procedures:** At the beginning of the year, you can have your classroom rules on posters, and students can graffiti them with examples of what these rules would look like on a daily basis. You can also have students reflect on what appropriate behavior looks like in various parts of the school by putting locations on paper and having them complete the same process.

Potential hurdles and how to prepare for them:

When students participate in Graffiti Walks, they often get carried away with the idea of graffiti. Your engaging activity can quickly turn into students feeling like their art was ruined, or the information on the posters can become very difficult to read. Make sure you have set expectations about respecting the work of others and remembering that although you love their creativity, you still need to be able to read their work.

PASS THE PAPER

How it works:

Students work in groups of 3 to 4. The teacher poses a question, topic, or idea, and each group is given a paper. It is important for the topic or question to have multiple answers or examples. Then, the teacher provides the group with an allotted amount of time, and they continuously pass the paper and keep adding answers, details, or ideas until the teacher calls time. After groups are done writing, teachers can collect the papers and debrief with the class, or you can provide time for each group to share what they have compiled.

Ways to implement Pass the Paper:

There are many variations of Pass the Paper that can be used to make your instruction more engaging and interactive for students.

- **Warm-Up/Closing:** You can use this format as a warm-up or closing activity for students to list or detail as much information or as many examples as they can on that day's topic. For example, if you were covering natural resources, students can use Pass the Paper to list types or examples of natural resources.

- **Application:** You can use this strategy to apply and practice during your instruction. For example, students can list rhyming words, equivalent fractions, or antonyms/synonyms.

- **Creative Writing:** Students can use this to collaboratively respond to a prompt. Each student starts with their own story, and when time is called, they pass the paper, read the new story, and add to it. At the end, each student gets their original story back and can read it to the group or the class. They can also use the story to move into an editing activity.

Potential hurdles and how to prepare for them:

You may find that students get impatient waiting for their turn or upset if their idea is taken before the paper gets to them.

These are great things to discuss before starting the activity, and patience is something we all have to learn!

FINAL THOUGHTS

Implementing cooperative practice in the classroom offers numerous benefits for both students and teachers. Students are significantly more engaged in their work when they are working with peers and when they have the opportunity to collaborate, discuss, and problem-solve together. Most of us can relate to this. If we are asked to run an after-school club or participate on a new committee, it often feels daunting and overwhelming. However, if you can collaboratively tackle these responsibilities with your partner teacher or someone else, it becomes much more appealing and less overwhelming. Your students feel these same emotions!

Cooperative practice also provides opportunities for students to strengthen their social skills. When they are asked to collaborate and work towards a common goal, they must learn to work together, merge different ideas and viewpoints, communicate, and resolve conflicts between each other. These skills help meet and strengthen the needs of the whole child instead of just the academic child.

Research has also shown time and time again that cooperative practice leads to improved student outcomes. Students learn well from each other, and when the classroom is set up this way, you, as the teacher, can meet all student needs and academic levels. Also, this type of learning environment fosters a sense of community and unity, meaning students actually want to be at school and be a part of the activities and learning that take place there on a daily basis.

Implementing cooperative practice time consistently and effectively helps improve the whole classroom while growing the whole child. You, as the teacher, are getting to be more intentional with your time and support; students are learning from each other; the classroom environment is starting to feel more like a family; and everyone is improving because we're all getting what we need. It can feel overwhelming at first, but start small, be consistent, and learn as you go, and you'll see a huge transformation.

INDEPENDENT PRACTICE

"Achievement is the outcome. The means to get there is student engagement." – Pedro Noguera

Independent practice is any portion of the instructional block when students are working on a task individually without direct teacher guidance or peer support. If students complete this at the end of a lesson, it provides them with an opportunity to apply the concepts or skills they have just learned and practiced, and it allows you, as the teacher, to determine their individual level of mastery. Independent practice can also be used as a quick warm-up activity to activate prior knowledge or during rotations for students to apply a particular skill.

Independent practice needs to be intentional and used with a clear objective in mind. We often see teachers jumping from whole group instruction right into independent practice. While this might be appropriate for certain projects or writing assignments, students typically need time to practice and process information cooperatively before they are ready to work independently. So, on a day-to-day basis, independent practice should only account for 10–25% of the instructional block.

The ultimate goal of independent practice is to provide the teacher with an understanding of each student's individual level of mastery of a particular skill or standard. We know maintaining student engagement during this time is often challenging, but in order to have an accurate depiction of your students' understanding, it is important to make this portion of the lesson as engaging as possible.

Some strategies that may be helpful when planning for independent practice are the following:

- **Relevant:** Activities need to be relevant and connected to the real world. If students have particular interests, this would be a good time to incorporate that as well.

- **Purpose:** Clearly define the objective and goal of the independent practice so students are informed. When students have a clear understanding of why they are completing something, they are typically more willing to stay on task and motivated to complete it.

- **Feedback:** Provide regularly timely feedback on the work students are completing during independent practice. This should be specific, constructive, and highlight areas for growth. Also, highlighting students' hard work can go a long way toward engaging them during this time and letting them know their effort isn't in vain.

- **Choice:** Students are much more engaged and willing to work when they feel like they have input into their learning. Small choices throughout the day can lead to large benefits for students and teachers.

- **Reflection & Self-Assessment:** Have students reflect on their progress and self-assess their work. Support them in evaluating their individual strengths and areas for improvement. Their reflections and goals may intrinsically motivate them and keep them engaged.

Remember, the key is to create a supportive and stimulating environment where learners feel motivated, challenged, and connected to the content. Adapt these strategies based on the specific needs and preferences of your learners.

THINGS TO REMEMBER AS YOU PLAN FOR INDEPENDENT PRACTICE

- **Short:** This should be the shortest portion of your instructional block. The assignment should only be as long as you need it to be in order to gain the appropriate information.

- **Intentional:** The assignments should be created to show you specific data. Think about what your lesson objective was and what you truly need to know in order to determine an accurate level of student mastery.

- **Relevant:** It should also be directly correlated with the material they just learned, not idle, busy work that is meant to fill time or get a grade.

STRATEGIES FOR INDEPENDENT PRACTICE

ENTRY TASKS

How it works:

Entry tasks are typically designed to activate students' prior knowledge of a topic or concept. These tasks can also be used to review a skill or revisit yesterday's lesson before jumping into that day's instruction.

Ways to implement entry tasks:

It is important to keep entry tasks brief, engaging, and connected to the content of the lesson. They should be designed to activate prior knowledge and stimulate students' thinking.

- **Question of the Day**: Pose a thought-provoking question related to the upcoming skill or a current event. Students can write their responses in a journal, on a whiteboard, or share them during your class discussion.

- **Visuals:** Display an image or clip and have students make observations, predictions, or connections relating to the topic or skill you are teaching. For example, if you are working on inferencing, you can show a picture and have students make as many inferences as they can.

- **Jamboard:** *Jamboard* is an online tool where all students have the ability to simultaneously share and respond. These can be used at the beginning of class for students to fill out a KWL chart, brainstorm ideas, or complete a bubble or concept map.

- **Brainteasers:** While this entry task may not be aligned with your daily academic objective, it is a fun, independent task that gets students settled after a transition. Many students enjoy the challenge of a brainteaser and will be engaged and ready to learn as you share the answer and move into your lesson. This can also set a positive tone for the rest of your block!

When I was in 8th grade, my science teacher started every class period with a brainteaser. We were on a bell schedule, and instead of going to the bathroom or chatting at our lockers, we eagerly got to class to see if we could solve the brainteaser before she revealed the answer. Many nights, this brainteaser became a topic at my family's dinner table. I am not sure if my teacher realized how impactful and engaging the brainteasers were or if she simply intended for them to buy her a few extra minutes to get ready for class. Regardless, they have become a core memory for me and impacted the way I planned entry tasks in my own classroom!

-Andra

Potential hurdles and how to prepare for them:

The biggest hurdle you must prepare for when giving entry tasks is time. Make sure your tasks are quick and don't eat into your instructional block. It is easy for students to get really into what you're talking about and want to have long discussions. Have a plan to let them know you're interested and love their sharing, but you have to move on.

EXIT TICKETS

How it works:

Exit tickets are short formative assessments used at the end of a lesson to gauge student understanding, gather feedback, or identify common misconceptions. They are meant to inform teachers and drive their day-to-day instructional decisions.

Information types that can be gained from exit tickets:

Exit tickets should be brief but informative. They can be in the form of multiple-choice questions, short-answer responses, reflections, problem-solving exercises, or even drawings. By analyzing students' exit tickets, you can gain a wealth of information.

- **Mastery:** The most common use of exit tickets is to gain an understanding of which students mastered a skill and who still needs practice or intervention. This information should be used to drive your upcoming lessons and can help you create leveled groups.

- **Misconceptions:** When assessing exit tickets, look for common trends and misconceptions. If there are specific mistakes or misunderstandings for the majority of students, it would be a good idea to start the following class by revisiting that area.

- **Reflection:** Exit tickets can be used for students to reflect and share what has benefited them, what they need to be successful, or how they are feeling about a particular skill or concept. This information can be very helpful as you plan for future lessons.

Potential hurdles and how to prepare for them:

While exit tickets can be very informative, there are some things to keep in mind. We know how valuable your instructional time is, and it can be challenging to fit exit tickets into your block. Keep the assignments brief and remind students that they only have an allotted amount of time to complete them. If they are struggling to complete the task in that amount of time, that should inform you that the skill has not been mastered and they need more support.

When attempting to keep your exit tickets brief and concise, it can be easy to leave out questions that give you valuable information. Think through the questions you're asking to ensure you're covering all aspects of your lesson. For example, if you're giving an exit ticket assessing your students' ability to subtract, make sure you have a question that involves no regrouping, regrouping across zeros, regrouping individual digits, and regrouping in the middle of a number. This will show you each misconception they could be making and help you know where to start the next day.

Many teachers feel overwhelmed by analyzing the data. This is meant to be informative and does not always have to be graded. You can take the papers or index cards and sort them by the number of questions students got correct or by students who made the same mistake, and use the piles to create your groups for the next

EXIT TICKET DATA ORGANIZER

day. Don't feel like this has to be a formal process or that you have to grade or respond to each individual exit ticket.

CHOICE BOARDS

How it works:

Choice boards are a simple strategy that can be used to provide students with choices of activities to complete that align with the lesson objective. The teacher creates a board of some sort with options for activities that meet that day's objective, and students complete a specified number of activities. When students feel like they have choices, they are often more motivated to complete assignments. These boards also give insight into your students' preferences. If you notice one type of activity is always chosen over others, you can use that information to drive other aspects of your classroom instruction.

Ways to implement Choice Boards:

There are many ways to implement choice boards in your classroom. Just make sure that the choices are compatible in time, rigor, and application. Remember to prioritize quality over quantity; if students choose 2 of 3 meaningful activities to complete, that is better than 4 of 9 subpar choices.

- **Current Skill:** Choice boards can be used to support and practice the current skill in a variety of ways.

- **Spiral Review:** Choice boards are a great way to review prior skills and topics.

- **Culminating Activity:** Having a choice board is a good alternative to a traditional study guide. You can embed videos, vocabulary activities, and practice within the board. Having students complete the board in a certain way (tic-tac-toe or choose a box from each column) can help ensure they get all types of review.

- **Learning Styles:** Using a choice board to meet the various learning styles in your classroom can be very beneficial. Some students may prefer to write a song to show mastery and understanding, while others would rather create slides or a poster.

<u>Potential hurdles and how to prepare for them:</u>

We know classrooms have mixed ability levels and interests, so as you create and implement choice boards in your classroom, think about ways that you can meet all your students' needs. You may find it helpful to vary the expectations for different students. One option for meeting the various ability levels is to have multiple choice boards assigned to students. This option requires the most work but can be very effective in ensuring each student gets what they need. Another option is to color-code the boxes on the choice board based on difficulty. If you color-code the activities as easy-yellow, moderate-blue, and difficult-orange (try not to always make green-high and red-low), your lower-level students may be required to choose 2 yellow boxes and 1 orange box, while your higher achieving students are required to choose 1 blue box and 2 orange boxes. The fast finishers in this activity can then pick another box of your choosing to complete.

Another challenge may be creating activities that are similar in the amount of time and effort they take to complete. If you find you have varying activities, you may want to consider a points system. With this type of choice board, each activity is assigned a number of points, and students have to complete enough to equal the established point goal. This means students may not have the same number of tasks, but the amount of time, effort, and application should be compatible.

ASSESSMENTS

We know assessments must be completed individually and require more time than we typically allocate for independent practice. However, when designing assessments, there are things you can keep in mind to make them engaging while still providing accurate data.

- **Student-Centered:** Think about your students' interests when you are writing word problems or choosing passages for an assessment. If students can connect and relate to the material, they are more engaged and motivated. Also, think about using your students' names and places in your community when you create scenarios, problems, or stories. If they know this is common practice, they will be eager to see if they have been included!

- **Flexibility:** Typically, when we hear the word "assessment," we think of a traditional, 20-question, multiple-choice test. While these types of tests have their place, think about times when students can show you their understanding through a different pathway. This can be in the form of a written essay, presentation, multimedia project, or poster. This leverages a student's learning style and creates a more engaging assessment.

- **Goal-Centered:** If students are actively working towards a goal, students will work hard to try and meet those goals. Think about rewarding goals that are met over time, encouraging students to become reflective and intrinsically motivated. Providing quick feedback helps support this as well.

FINAL THOUGHTS

Independent practice is a valuable component of the learning process that requires students to work individually and apply what they have learned while providing the teacher with meaningful and necessary information. It provides students with valuable opportunities to apply and reinforce their knowledge and skills, fostering autonomy, critical thinking, and self-regulation. By engaging in independent practice, students become active participants in their own learning and develop the resilience and self-discipline needed for lifelong learning. Although it is not the most engaging portion of the instructional block, it is through independent practice that students can truly internalize and make meaningful connections with the content they are learning. The information teachers gain from this work is informative and imperative to creating a classroom that meets the needs of all learners.

Overall, independent practice provides teachers with valuable data, opportunities for individualized support, and insights that inform instruction and promote student growth. It allows teachers to tailor their teaching to meet students' needs, foster self-directed learning, and continuously improve their instructional practices.

BEYOND THE BLOCK ENGAGEMENT STRATEGIES

"Provide an uncommon experience for your students, and they will reward you with an uncommon effort and attitude." —Dave Burgess

We have covered many engagement strategies that are specific to one area of the instructional block, but there are other strategies that don't fit into one portion. Some of these activities require your entire block or even your whole day, while others can be adapted to fit the needs of your classroom.

The strategies we will cover throughout this chapter are classroom transformations, flexible classroom environments, and centers and rotations. These strategies require a significant amount of time and planning, and they each have their own expectations and procedures that will need to be thought through, introduced, and modeled before they can be implemented successfully.

CLASSROOM TRANSFORMATIONS

Classroom transformations can be the ultimate engagement tool for your classroom. You can turn your room into a new adventure, place, or experience for students. By transforming the physical space, decor, and activities to reflect the chosen theme, educators can spark students' curiosity and create memorable learning experiences. This strategy takes a lot of work and planning, but the rewards are worth it! Transformations are great for difficult units when you need students to be focused and engaged. They are also great to do during the long, cold months of the winter, so students forget they are even in the classroom. Transformations can be successful across all grade levels and content areas. Depending on the objective of your lesson, transformations can be centered around a theme, based on an experience, or aligned to a topic or unit you are teaching.

Tips and Ideas for Any Transformation

- **Decor and Set-up:** Transform your classroom with decorations that reflect the chosen theme. Use posters, banners, cutouts, and props to create an immersive environment. Think about the activities students will be doing and how your room can be set up to best facilitate them. You don't have to always have fancy or expensive items. Remember, these are kids; it doesn't take a lot of material things to impress them. It's all about the buildup and commitment from you. Speaking from experience, I once pulled off a "circus" with a circus tent picture projected on the board, music playing in the background, and a masking tape tightrope. Don't overthink it!

- **Dress and Role Play:** Encourage students to dress up in attire related to the theme or assign roles for role-playing activities. This helps students immerse themselves in the theme and enhances their understanding and engagement. For instance, if your transformation is boot camp, encourage students to wear camouflage or green colors, boots, or a hat. If your theme doesn't lend itself to items students would have at home, you can let them create their own name tags or hats as an entry task.

- **Pique Interest and Anticipation:** On the days leading to your transformation, start to pique students' interest so they are excited and anticipating the big event. This can be done by asking them to dress up the next day, but don't tell them why. You can give students a ticket to enter the room before the transformation day or prior to that lesson. You can also tell them they need to clear their space before they leave because you are changing the room for a surprise the next day. Regardless of how you pique their interest and curiosity, the ultimate goal is for students to be excited and eager to participate.

- **Alternate Activity:** As you plan for transformations, have an alternate activity prepared for students who impede the learning of other students. When you introduce the transformation, clearly state this expectation so they understand. The goal is for students to be so immersed in the activity that these issues don't arise. However, you need to be prepared if they do!

THEMED TRANSFORMATIONS

Themed transformations base your lessons and activities for the day around a common theme. This is the easiest type of transformation to use for an entire grade level, team, or school. The theme may relate to any subject, time of year, holiday, or student interest.

Examples:

- Christmas Tree Farm
- Haunted House
- Glow in the Dark

- Football Game
- Beach Party
- Boot Camp

EXPERIENCE TRANSFORMATIONS

Experience transformations provide your students with an experience. They are more hands-on than the other transformations and are great to use when students are working on a skill that is typically seen as boring and unengaging. These transformations are a great way to expose students to opportunities they may not have or provide connections to a real-life experience of the strategy or skill. If done correctly. It is almost like students are getting an extra field trip!

Examples:

- Hospital: Surgery on contractions or inequalities
- Construction Zone: Adding prefixes/suffixes, creating animal habitats, subdividing polygons
- Detective Theme: Inferences, word problems
- Farmer's Market: Money, decimals, advertisement writing

ALIGNED TRANSFORMATIONS

Aligned transformations bring to life the content you are currently teaching. These transformations allow students to have experiences similar to the topics they're learning about; they can be transported to a different time or place that supports your unit. Aligned transformations bridge the other types. These transformations last the whole day and support a cross-curricular classroom.

Examples:

- Civil War
- Space Expedition
- Oceans
- Industrial Revolution

FLEXIBLE CLASSROOM ENVIRONMENT

Gone are the days of all classrooms being rows of desks and chairs. Students may feel more comfortable and ready to learn if they have flexibility in their classroom environment. This will also give them a sense of ownership and belonging.

Creating a flexible classroom environment involves intentional design and organization to support student engagement, collaboration, and choice. By providing a flexible environment, your classroom will become student-centered rather than teacher-centered. This shift will create a sense of pride and ownership for your students.

SEATING

Flexible seating gives students choices in seat placement and type. These choices give students autonomy and cater to their individual needs and learning styles.

When planning for flexible seating, there are some things you need to think through in order to maximize your space and benefits.

- **Assess your space:** Evaluate the physical layout of your classroom and identify areas that can be modified or rearranged to accommodate flexible seating and learning options. Consider the size of your space, the available furniture, and the flow of movement within the classroom.

- **Furniture Choices:** Decide what types of flexible seating you will be able to offer your students. There is a large variety of seating choices out there, such as stools, rocking chairs, standing desks, carpet squares, lap desks, exercise or stability balls, or bean bags. This can easily become very expensive and overwhelming. Think about starting small and requesting funds or donations from your school or local community. There are also many grants that can help you transform this aspect of your environment. When choosing your initial pieces, consider the students you currently have and what would be most beneficial to them. For example, if they are active and fidgety, exercise balls or standing desks might be a good first option.

- **Modeling and Establishing Expectations:** As you introduce students to flexible seating, you will have to model appropriate use and set expectations. Students are often excited to try any new classroom additions and will need guidelines for how to appropriately use them, choose them, and care for them. It may be chaotic and distracting the first few days, but remind students that this type of seating is intended to support their learning, so if a seating choice is distracting, it is probably not the best option for them. Ideally, students would be able to choose their best seating option; however, if you notice students continually making poor choices or know that a student is particularly successful in a certain seating option, it is appropriate for you to assign permanent seating arrangements.

When I was teaching fourth grade, I applied for a grant to receive flexible seating for my classroom. I was awarded the grant and provided 24 orange yoga balls for my students. I was excited for my students, and they were beyond eager for them to arrive. At this point in time, flexible seating wasn't as common as it is today. My teammates thought I was crazy and were convinced that my students would be bouncing all over my room instead of listening to me. Yes, I had students who bounced, and I had students who had to make other choices some days, but for the most part, they were fantastic. Like everything else in life, the honeymoon phase wore off, and eventually they were just part of the classroom and our daily routine. I started with four yoga balls in our small group, where I could monitor, redirect, and remind students about the expectations. As students became comfortable with the balls and my expectations, I added them to different desks around the room until all twenty-four had a home. The overall benefits of flexible seating far outweighed the hurdles of getting them set up, and I loved having them set up in my classroom!

-Andra

ORGANIZATION

Having an organized room is not only visually appealing to students, but it also creates an environment that is conducive to learning and predictable. Students tend to thrive in structured environments, and as the teacher, you are able to focus on being creative and engaging.

- **Organized Student Spaces:** Create different learning spaces within your classroom to support various learning activities and preferences. Have areas where students can work independently and areas for group work. For example, you don't want a group of students trying to work at one desk, so have a table designated for collaborative work that students know they can go to.

- **Organized Materials and Storage:** Create storage solutions that allow for easy access to materials and resources. Use labeled bins, shelves, or carts to store extra supplies or manipulatives that students use on a regular basis. Have designated areas for things like turning in work, getting their missing assignments, or finding a fast-finisher activity. Encourage students to take responsibility for maintaining the cleanliness and organization of the classroom.

ATMOSPHERE

By knowing your students and their learning styles, you can create an atmosphere that they find positive and appealing. You can create this type of atmosphere by incorporating various types of lighting or music. Think about your students as you design and decorate the classroom. Consider allowing them to have input and ownership. Give students opportunities to create artwork or motivational posters and have a designated space for showcasing student work.

Remember to regularly reflect on the effectiveness of your flexible classroom environment. Seek feedback from students about their experiences, make adjustments, and adapt the environment based on evolving learning needs. Creating a flexible classroom environment is an ongoing process that requires flexibility, adaptability, and open communication with your students. By providing students with choices in their seating and working environment while also ensuring a level of organization and predictability, you can create a dynamic and student-centered classroom that supports their diverse needs and fosters engagement.

CENTERS AND ROTATIONS

Classroom centers and rotations are engaging ways to provide students with multiple ways to interact and apply a skill. They can include teacher-led groups or spiral review activities. The purpose of classroom centers and rotations is to provide students with hands-on, interactive experiences that promote active learning, collaboration, and independent thinking.

Using centers and rotations can seem overwhelming and hectic, and many teachers may feel like they require too much planning. However, with explicit expectations and intentional organization, this strategy can quickly become part of your daily routine. The benefits of centers and rotations are endless, and once students become accustomed to the practices and expectations, they love the variety, movement, and collaboration that come along with this style of instruction. To successfully plan, organize, and implement centers and rotations, you must be intentional and flexible.

PLANNING

As you plan for centers and rotations, keep in mind your objective for the lesson. There is no magic number of rotations that students should visit in a day, so put more focus on the quality of the centers instead of time constraints and quantity. Whether you set them up to visit three centers in one day or five over two days, what matters is what they are learning and gaining from each rotation.

Rotation activities can be differentiated and scaffolded to meet the needs of your students. This is imperative so that groups and students can work without the support of an adult. It provides an opportunity to correct misunderstandings and bridge learning gaps and misconceptions.

GROUPING

Another big thing to keep in mind as you plan is how you will group and schedule students. The best way to group students is by ability level. The lowest group should start with you, and the highest can begin at a more independent rotation, where they have the ability to be successful without additional support. This allows you to extend them at the end, when the lower students are more prepared to work without you. Another option would be for you to set up your centers so there is no teacher-led group. This allows you to follow the lowest group and provide support when necessary. You are also able to facilitate and observe what is taking place in the other groups and provide immediate feedback and correction.

PHYSICAL ORGANIZATION

Organization and procedures are more important with this strategy than any other. There are so many moving parts during centers and rotations that it is easy to overlook key elements that help them run smoothly. Some organizational tips to keep in mind are the following:

- Have a basket or bucket that contains all the copies and supplies students need to complete that center.

- Designate spaces with appropriate seating for each center activity. This helps keep all materials where they need to be for upcoming groups, and it helps support your management.

- Define what work needs to be turned in for a grade and where. Not every center needs to have something physical or graded. Some centers can use task cards and game boards, reusable matching activities, games in sheet protectors, or computer activities.

- Many of your centers can be reused for other skills, in the future for spiral review, or saved for the following school year. Keep them organized in buckets or totes so you can avoid having to remake things. Once you create a large supply of centers, all you have to do is pull them out and you're ready to go. It may also be helpful to use cardstock and laminate these center activities as you make them.

I invested an enormous amount of time into creating centers that could be used year after year at the beginning of my teaching career. I had a wonderful mentor who showed me their value from the beginning and a fantastic paraprofessional who spent countless hours helping me laminate, cut, and organize all their pieces. I ultimately had multiple centers for every unit that I taught, which were used as practice and spiral review as the year progressed. I tiered most of my centers as I made them to ensure they would meet the various ability levels of my students. Every year following, all I had to do was make copies of an answer sheet or have students work on notebook paper and pull centers out of my cabinets. This saved me so much time with planning and creating lessons! I knew my material was aligned, leveled, and engaging, and I could reuse it day after day, year after year. Once I moved into a coaching position, these kept growing and eventually spanned across four different grade levels. I took the time one summer to organize all the games and activities into similar buckets and to label each bucket with what it included and the grade levels that aligned with them. While this took a lot of time upfront, they became easily accessible to anyone who wanted to use them, held up to the wear and tear due to the forethought in their creation, and are still being used daily, many years later!

– Sarah

Implementation:

Before you are fully able to run and implement centers, there are several procedures, tools, and resources you will need in place to make them as efficient and successful as possible. Before you start using centers and rotations on a daily basis, take time to model and practice with students using activities that are not academic. This can be done with board games, puzzles, or SEL activities. Once students know how rotations work, what smooth transitions look and sound like, and the expectations of working with a group, they will be ready to dive into academic and skill-based rotations.

- Create a visual for students to see what center they are assigned to and where they will be going next.

- Have a fast-finisher in place for students who finish their center activity before the time is up. We all know downtime lends itself to behavior problems, so having an established fast-finisher helps with this. Consider a fast-finisher that is challenging and interesting, such as "finding the mistake" or a puzzle activity. Fast-finishers should not just be extra work because typically the students who are going to get to them will be students who need to be extended.

- You will need to model and set clear expectations for students so they know what an effective day of rotations looks like. Students should know how to: participate in rotation activities; transition between centers; stop where they are and quickly clean up; prepare their space for the next group; and turn in their work. If you notice these areas need to be revisited, take the time to stop and practice. You may feel like you are losing time, but in reality, you are gaining time, and in the end, the gains will be beneficial for everyone.

FINAL THOUGHTS

Broad student engagement strategies provide a wide range of student-centered activities that support a dynamic and interactive classroom. These activities shift the focus of the classroom from the teacher as the sole provider of knowledge to the students owning and experiencing their own learning. We are not blind to the fact that many of these take a lot of time, effort, and preparation, but we have also seen the gains. Once these routines and strategies have been established, the majority of the work is done, allowing you to focus on other tasks. Many of these engagement strategies provide students with hands-on, real-world experiences that go beyond the classroom and have a lifelong impact.

THE MAGIC OF ENGAGEMENT

"When students are engaged, magic happens in the classroom." –Todd Whitaker

By now, you know how passionately we feel about student engagement! Engagement can create magical classrooms where students are excited to learn and happy to be there. There are many misconceptions about engagement that we want to debunk while acknowledging the fact that student engagement is not truly magic and can't fix all the challenges that come with teaching.

THE MAGICAL CLASSROOM

Right now, you are probably focused on how you will start planning for student engagement and embedding strategies into your instructional block. That is an exciting place to be; however, the true magic of student engagement occurs when you get beyond mere participation and surface-level engagement and gain an active mental and emotional investment from your students. When you reach this stage of engagement, you are able to engage students at deeper levels.

- **Emotional Engagement:** Emotional engagement refers to students' feelings and attitudes toward their learning experiences. When students feel a sense of belonging, motivation, and enjoyment in the classroom, their attitude changes from uninterested and skeptical to excited and happy to see what they get to do today. Questions change from What do I have to do today? to What do I get to do today? You will start to see students who were typically resistant to certain subjects or activities transition into students who are willing and eager to take risks and try new things.

- **Behavioral Engagement:** Behavioral engagement not only refers to seeing a decrease in undesirable behaviors but also an increase in students' active participation and involvement in learning activities. It encompasses behaviors such as attending class regularly, actively participating in discussions, completing assignments on time, and seeking help when needed. Students who have reached this depth have a willingness to put forth the effort required for learning.

- **Cognitive Engagement:** Cognitive engagement refers to students' mental investment and the effort they put into their learning. It reaches higher-order thinking skills such as critical thinking, problem-solving, and a deep understanding of the content. When students are cognitively engaged, they actively process information, make connections, ask questions, and apply their knowledge to real-world situations. As students reach this level, you may see them begin to transfer their learning outside the classroom and make true real-world connections.

- **Social Engagement:** Social engagement refers to students' interaction and collaboration with peers and teachers. Students will begin to recognize their peers' areas of strength and leverage and respect their diversity. The classroom will begin to transform into a true community where students support and rely on each other in order for everyone to grow.

MAGICAL TIPS AND MISCONCEPTIONS

As you create a classroom environment that maximizes student engagement and values your time as an educator, we want to share some tips and debunk common misconceptions that often keep teachers from focusing on student engagement.

- **Time:** We often hear teachers say that they don't have time for student engagement. There is a common misconception that student engagement takes more time during the instructional block and in planning. We aren't here to say that it doesn't take time to plan and implement activities that are engaging for students. In the beginning, it will take more time, but if you think about creating resources that can be reused throughout subject areas and your year, once they are created, the work will be done. You may need different task cards, practice problems, or questions for the current skill or objective, but the base of your activity will already be complete. For example, if you create game boards and laminate them, they can be reused for any lesson.

- **Chaos:** Many teachers correlate student engagement with chaos. They envision an unorganized classroom with no order that is loud and unruly. When we think of student engagement, we envision controlled chaos. Yes, students will be talking with each other and participating in various activities, but there will be order and organization. You can gauge your chaos by the relevance of the conversations and the excitement surrounding your activity. By setting expectations and procedures, you can avoid chaos, and you will probably be surprised at how engaged students are in their learning. In fact, we would argue that chaotic classrooms are the result of bored students who don't have procedures and expectations in place. This is why consistently reinforcing and maintaining expectations is vital to success.

- **Grading:** A common misconception is that in order for student work to be meaningful, it must be collected and graded. While grades are certainly necessary, some activities are only meant for practice. It's okay for students to complete rotations or partner activities that you don't collect (and might even throw away); use an exit ticket to determine their independent mastery levels and to guide the instruction the following day. As you are deciding what tasks to grade, remember that grades should reflect a student's true ability level and should be taken after they have had time to practice and apply that skill.

- **Entertainment:** Engagement is often pictured as a high-energy classroom environment where the teacher is required to entertain students. While excited teachers and stimulating activities are great, true engagement goes beyond that. It is about having a student-centered environment where students are actively applying skills and ideas in meaningful, relevant ways. When true engagement is reached, the teacher gets to become more of a facilitator, and the students are doing the work.

- **Expense:** Another common misconception is that student engagement means you have to spend a large amount of money on supplies and activities. While there are many ways you can spend your money making your classroom more engaging, this is not necessary for success. Engagement comes from your knowledge of students' interests and likes and your ability to translate that into relevant, meaningful learning experiences. Expense does not equal engagement!

OUTSIDE THE MAGIC

While maximizing student engagement may remedy many of the challenges you are facing in your classroom, it is not the magic cure for everything. There are several challenges that must be addressed outside of creating an engaging classroom environment.

- **Structural Challenges:** There are many structures in place in a school that are outside your control. For example, class sizes, instructional time, programs, and curriculum. These structural issues limit your ability to engage students and provide the time you need to maximize effectiveness. Although this can be frustrating, think creatively about small changes or adaptations you can make that would allow you to engage students. You might be surprised at what an impact even a small change can have.

- **External Challenges:** Unfortunately, factors outside the classroom can affect students' engagement levels, social interactions, and academic performance. Socioeconomic status, family support, personal circumstances, and other external factors can significantly impact students' mindsets and how they come to school each day. Addressing these external factors often requires resources and support beyond your classroom. This can include support from the administration, counselors, families, or outside support agencies.

FINAL THOUGHTS

At this point, we have inundated you with tips, strategies, personal stories, ideas, misconceptions, and advice. As you take what you need from this book for implementation in your own classroom, it is important for reflection to be a big part of your upcoming journey. Some things you try may be successful, and others may flop, but failing forward is part of the process. Take the time to reflect on what's going well, what changes you need to make, and how your students are responding to the changes so you can create a classroom where everyone enjoys being and gets what they need. Student engagement does not happen overnight; it takes constant reflection, adaptation, and creativity. Engagement changes with each unit, student, and school year, so you must keep a constant pulse on your classroom and be flexible. We are excited for you to begin your journey to student engagement and bash the boredom in your classroom!

ABOUT THE AUTHORS

Andra Bostic is a former instructional coach and classroom teacher. She has an elementary education degree from Virginia Tech, a master's degree in early childhood education from Liberty University, and most recently an endorsement in administrative supervision and leadership from Longwood University.

Andra currently co-owns Tailored Education, an educational consulting company that specializes in supporting new and international teachers and provides custom professional development. She lives in Lynchburg, Virginia, with her husband Will and their three kids, Sydney, Myleigh, and Mason.

Sarah Murphy is a former instructional coach and classroom teacher. She has an elementary education degree from Lynchburg College and a master's degree in administrative supervision and leadership from Liberty University.

Sarah currently co-owns Tailored Education, an educational consulting company that specializes in supporting new and international teachers and provides custom professional development. She lives in Montvale, Virginia, with her husband Scottie and their daughter, Ellie.

Contact Us at Tailored Education
Email: *educationtailored@gmail.com*
Webpage: *www.educationtailored.com*
Facebook: */EducationTailored*

www.ingramcontent.com/pod-product-compliance
Lightning Source LLC
Chambersburg PA
CBHW070715130626
46553CB00005B/2000